The Kingman Comprehension Series

Elementary Level 3

Dr. Alice Kingman

PARTRIDGE

To order additional copies of this book, contact
Toll Free +65 3165 7531 (Singapore)
Toll Free +60 3 3099 4412 (Malaysia)
orders.singapore@partridgepublishing.com

www.partridgepublishing.com/singapore

CONTENTS

Acknowledgements vii
To Teacher and Parent ix

Ali Baba and the Forty Thieves 1
Belling the Cat 3
Twinkle, Twinkle, Little Star 5
The Frog Prince 7
Winnie the Pooh 9
The Elves and the Shoemaker 11
The Slave and the Lion 13
The Dog and the Cook 15
The Story of the Fisherman 17
The Journal: Or Birthday Gifts 19
The Story of Goldilocks and the Three Bears 21
Buster Bear Goes Fishing 23
What Is Pink? 25
The Little Mermaid Story 27
The Poor Sick Mother 29
Hansel and Gretel 31
The Velveteen Rabbit 33
Cinderella 35
Beauty and the Beast 37
My Father's Dragon 39

Acknowledgements

First, I would like to thank Jazzy, the illustrator of the Kingman Comprehension Series, for her beautiful artistic drawings which bring every story she has worked on to life.

My great appreciation is also to be extended to my two daughters, Stephanie and Audrey, who helped me from the very beginning in the typing and formatting of questions for every reading passage.

A big thank you to my beloved husband, Matt, for his continuous support, encouragement and professional assistance in the computerised structuring of the book.

I am also grateful to all my students for their contributions to this project, working on different passages, testing out questions and providing invaluable feedback.

With no reservation, my heartfelt gratitude goes to my beloved late father, Joseph, who spared no effort in teaching me English since I was seven years old.

Thank you to all other members of my family who spurred me on to take this big step in realising my dreams of becoming an English-language author. I thank them for their love and patience throughout the whole process. Thank you to my wonderful church family as well for their uplifting prayers and support.

Last but not least, I thank God, my Heavenly Father, every day for His unfailing presence and spiritual guidance, without which this project would not have happened.

To Teacher and Parent

In my lifelong career as an English-language teacher, I have often been disappointed and discouraged to find questions set for comprehension passages stressing speedy location of answers or meticulous reproduction of the text. The formulated questions seldom encourage students to read between the lines or genuinely understand the writer's choice of diction and intention of writing. In other words, students are often deprived of opportunities to think out of the box and explore implied meanings and examine the purpose of sentence structure.

Hence, it has always been my ambition to produce a comprehension series that can sharpen students' skills in analytical discernment. The Kingman Comprehension Series comprises high-interest selections of different literary genres from classics to renowned children's literature including fables, folk and fairy tales, poems, legends, myths as well as modern realistic fictions. It is my hope that students will find the works of the outstanding authors in the books not only enjoyable to work on but also interesting enough to spark further independent reading among themselves.

Ali Baba and the Forty Thieves

Albert Goodwin

In a town of Persia lived two brothers, sons of poor men: one named Cassim, the other, Ali Baba. Cassim, the elder, married a wife with considerable fortune and lived at his ease, but the wife of Ali Baba was as poor as himself. They dwelt in a mean cottage in the suburbs, and he maintained his family by cutting wood. Ali Baba was in the forest preparing to load his asses with the wood he had cut when he saw a troop of horsemen approaching. He hastily climbed a large thick tree and hid himself among the branches. Ali Baba counted forty of them. Each took a loaded portmanteau from his horse and, turning to the rock, said, 'Open, Sesame.' Immediately a door opened. The robbers passed in when the door shut itself. In a short time, the door opened again. The robbers came out and said, 'Shut, Sesame.' The door instantly closed. Ali Baba ventured down and, approaching the rock, said, 'Open Sesame.' Immediately the door flew open. He brought his asses and took as many bags of gold coins as they could carry.

Ali Baba told his brother the secret of the cave. Cassim rose early next morning and set out with ten mules loaded with great chests. He found the rock and, having said, 'Open Sesame,' gained admission, where he found more treasures than he expected, which made him forget the word that caused the door to open. Presently he heard the sound of horses' feet, <u>which</u> he concluded to be the robbers.'

Answer the following questions.

1. Cassim and Ali Baba were _____ who lived in a town of _____.

2. The wife of Cassim was

    a. wealthy
    b. poor

3. Was Ali Baba's wife richer than Ali Baba? Which line tells us that?

4. What was the occupation of Ali Baba?

5. The word that means 'coming near' in the first paragraph is _____.

6. What did Ali Baba take after he had entered the cave?

7. Why did Cassim take with him great chests?

8. Would Cassim be overjoyed upon stepping into the cave? Why or why not?

9. What made Cassim forget the word that caused the door to open?

    a. fear
    b. hatred
    c. sadness
    d. greed

10. The relative pronoun 'which' in the last sentence is referring to _____

_____.

Read on:

Translated by Antoine Gallard and published between 1839 and 1842, 'Ali Baba and the Forty Thieves' is one of the stories in *One Thousand and One Nights*. It features a poor woodcutter, Ali Baba, who has a most unkind brother, Cassim. Ali Baba, by chance, watches forty thieves hiding their looted treasures in a cave, which opens to the verbal command 'Open, Sesame!' The fortune and fate of the two brothers are revealed to differ dramatically at the end of the story.

Belling the Cat

Aesop

The mice met in council to figure out how to defeat the Cat. One suggested a bell for the Cat to warn them.

Problem: Nobody would volunteer to bell the Cat.

It is easy to propose impossible remedies.

Long ago, the mice had a general council to consider what measures they could take to outwit their common enemy, the Cat. Some said this, and some said that, but at last, a young mouse got up and said he had a proposal to make which he thought would meet the case. 'You will all agree,' said he, 'that our chief danger consists in the sly and treacherous manner in which the enemy approaches us. Now, if we could receive some signal of her approach, we could easily escape from her. I venture, therefore, to propose that a small bell be procured, and attached by a ribbon round the neck of the Cat. By this means we should always know when she was about, and could easily retire while she was in the neighbourhood.'

This proposal met with general applause until an old mouse got up and said, 'That is all very well, but who is to bell the Cat?' The mice looked at one another and nobody spoke. Then the old mouse said, 'It is easy to propose impossible remedies.'

Answer the following questions.

1. Which two words tell us that this story happened in the distant past?

2. Who is the enemy of the mice?

3. Underline the part of the sentence in the second last paragraph that tells us that the mice disagree with one another.

4. What did the young mouse do to meet the case?

5. What two adjectives are used to describe the Cat?

6. The young mouse believed that if they could receive some _____ of the _____ of the Cat, they could easily _____ from her.

7. What two objects were needed to carry out the plan?

8. Underline the phrase (three words in the last paragraph) which means 'clapping of hands to show approval'.

9. Who was going to bell the Cat?

10. Arrange the following sentences in the correct sequence:

    _____ The proposal met with general applause.
    _____ A general council meeting was held.
    _____ No mice were ready to bell the Cat.
    _____ A young mouse made a proposal.

11. Underline the correct word.

    The story 'Belling the Cat' is a memoir / fable / legend, because there is a strong moral behind it.

Read on:

In the fable 'Belling the Cat', written by Aesop (620–564 BC), a nest of mice is debating on how to abate the threat posed by the haunting presence of a formidable cat. One of them suggests tying a bell around the neck of the cat. The proposal is well applauded, but silence ensues when the council of mice is asked who is going to carry out this risky, dangerous plan.

Twinkle, Twinkle, Little Star

Jane Taylor

Twinkle, twinkle, little star,
How I wonder what you are!
Up above the world so high,
Like a diamond in the sky.

When the blazing sun is gone,
When <u>he</u> nothing shines upon,
Then you show your little light,
Twinkle, twinkle, all the night.

Then the traveller in the dark
Thanks you for your tiny spark,
How could he see where to go,
If you did not twinkle so?

In the dark blue sky you keep,
Often through my curtains peep
For you never shut your eye,
Till the sun is in the sky.

As you bright and tiny spark
Lights the traveller in the dark,
Though I know not what you are,
Twinkle, twinkle, little star.

Answer the following questions.

1. The poem is most probably written from the perspective of

    a. a baby
    b. a child
    c. a teenager
    d. an adult

2. What is the star compared to in the first stanza?

3. Which word in the second stanza means 'very hot'?

4. In the verse 'When <u>he</u> nothing shines upon', 'he' is referring to _____ _____.

5. According to the third stanza of the poem, why is the traveller thankful for the star?

6. Underline the only question the poet asked the star.

7. Which of the following is not a characteristic of the star?

    a. It never shuts its eye.
    b. It is bright and tiny.
    c. It comes out in the daytime to twinkle.
    d. It shows a traveller the way.

8. Does the poet understand the star fully? Quote one verse to support your answer.

9. Arrange the following sentences in the correct sequence according to the poem:

    _____ The star shows its light when the bright sun is gone.
    _____ The poet wonders what the star is.
    _____ The star shows the traveler the way in the dark.
    _____ The star shines like a diamond in the sky.

Read on:

'Twinkle, Twinkle Little Star' is a popular English lullaby with its lyrics based on 'The Star' written by Jane Taylor in the early nineteenth century.

Published in 1806, the poem praises the presence of a star shining brightly and with dignity in the dark. The shimmering of the little star often guides one along one's way in different and seemingly insignificant scenarios.

The popular melody of the lullaby is from 'Ah! Vous dirai-je, Maman!', a French children's song that means 'Oh! Shall I tell you, Mama!' It carries the same tune as several other popular children's songs like 'The Alphabet Song' and 'Baa, Baa, Black Sheep'.

The Frog Prince

The Brothers Grimm

One fine evening, a young princess put on her bonnet and clogs and went out to take a walk by herself in a wood, and when she came to a cool spring of water with a rose in the middle of it, she sat herself down to rest a while. Now she had a golden ball in her hand, which was her favourite plaything, and she was always tossing it up into the air and catching it again as it fell.

After a time she threw it up so high that she missed catching it as it fell, and the ball bounded away and tolled along the ground until at last it fell down into the spring. The princess looked into the spring after her ball, but it was very deep, so deep that she could not see the bottom of it. She began to cry and said, 'Alas! If I could only get my ball again, I would give all my fine clothes and jewels, and everything that I have in the world.'

Whilst she was speaking, a frog put its head out of the water and said, 'Princess, why do you weep so bitterly?'

'Alas!' said she, 'what can you do for me, you nasty frog? My golden ball has fallen into the spring.'

The frog said, 'I do not want your pearls, and jewels, and fine clothes, but if you will love me, and let me live with you and eat from off your golden plate, and sleep on your bed, I will bring you your ball again.'

What nonsense, thought the princess. *This silly frog is talking! He can never even get out of the spring to visit me though he may be able to get my ball for me, and therefore I will tell him he shall have what he asks.*

Answer the following questions.

1. The princess was wearing a _____ on her head and _____ on her feet.

2. What grew in the middle of the spring of water?

    a. a rose
    b. a lily
    c. lotus

3. Underline the expression (three words in the first paragraph) that tells us that the princess likes her golden ball a lot.

4. Is a golden ball made of gold?

5. Where did the golden ball go when the princess failed to catch it?

6. Could the princess see the golden ball in the spring? Why or why not?

7. Which was not one of the things the princess offered to give to the frog for his help?

    a. fine clothes
    b. jewels
    c. the golden ball

8. Underline the one word that tells us that the princess was crying very hard.

9. True or False:

    a. The frog wanted the princess to love him. _____
    b. The frog wanted to eat from her silver plate. _____

10. Why did the princess think the frog's wish would not come true?

Read on:

'The Frog Prince', a classical fairy tale found in *Grimm's Fairy Tales* (an 1812 anthology of German folklore), is a story about a prince who lives in a pond after being turned into a frog by an evil witch. A chance encounter with a playful princess offers the prince an opportunity to break the spell to become a prince again.

Winnie the Pooh

A. A. Milne

Piglet felt very miserable and didn't know what to say. He was still opening his mouth to begin something, and then deciding that it wasn't any good saying that, when he heard a shout from the other side of the river, and there was Pooh.

'Many happy returns of the day,' called out Pooh, forgetting that he had said it already.

'Thank you, Pooh, I'm having them,' said Eeyore gloomily.

'I've brought you a little present,' said Pooh excitedly.

'I've had <u>it</u>,' said Eeyore.

Pooh had now splashed across the stream to Eeyore, and Piglet was sitting a little way off, his head in his paws, snuffling to himself.

'It's a Useful Pot,' said Pooh. 'Here it is. And it's got "A Very Happy Birthday with love from Pooh" written on it. That's what all that writing is. And it's for putting things in. There!'

When Eeyore saw the pot, he became quite excited.

'Why!' he said. 'I believe my Balloon will just go into that Pot!'

'Oh, no, Eeyore,' said Pooh. 'Balloons are much too big to go into Pots. What you do with a balloon is, you hold the balloon.'

Answer the following questions.

1. Piglet didn't know what to say because he felt

    a. very unhappy
    b. very tired
    c. very excited

2. Did Piglet end up saying something before he saw Pooh?

3. Where was Pooh when Piglet saw him?

4. 'Many happy returns of the day' is another way of saying

    a. 'Good morning'
    b. 'Have a nice day'
    c. 'Happy birthday'

5. While Eeyore was feeling gloomy, Pooh was feeling _____.

6. 'I've had it,' said Eeyore. What is 'it' referring to?

7. What sound did Piglet make while sitting a little way off?

8. What present did Pooh give to Eeyore? What was it for?

9. Was Eeyore happy to see the Pot? How do you know?

10. According to Pooh, why can't balloons go into Pots?

Read on:

Winnie the Pooh, also called *Pooh Bear* and *Pooh*, was created by English writer A. A. Milne. The story centres around heart-warming and fun episodes that take place among a fictional teddy bear and his dear friends: Christopher Robin, Piglet, Eeyore, Owl, Rabbit, Roo and Kanga.

All the stories created around the main character, Pooh, can be read independently as most of the plots do not carry between stories except for stories 9 and 10.

Winnie the Pooh has been translated into more than fifty languages, with the characters in the book being adapted into other media, most notably by Disney.

The Elves and the Shoemaker

The Brothers Grimm

A shoemaker, by no fault of his own, had become so poor that at last he had nothing left but leather for one pair of shoes. So, in the evening, he cut out the shoes which he wished to begin to make the next morning, and as he had a good conscience, he lay down quietly in his bed, commended himself to God, and fell asleep. In the morning, after he had said his prayers, and was just going to sit down to work, the two shoes stood quite finished on his table. He was astounded and knew not what to say to it. He took the shoes in his hands to observe them closer, and they were so neatly made that there was not one bad stitch.

The following morning, too, he found the four pairs made, and so it went on constantly; what he cut out in the evening was finished by the morning so that he soon had his honest independence again and at last became a wealthy man. Not it befell that one evening not long before Christmas, when the man had been cutting out, he said to his wife, before going to bed, 'What think you if we were to stay up tonight to see who it is that lends us this helping hand?' The woman liked the idea and lit a candle, and then they hid themselves in a corner of the room behind some clothes which were hanging up there and watched. When it was midnight, two pretty little men came, sat down by the shoemaker's table, took all the work which was cut out before them and began to stitch, sew and hammer so skilfully and so quickly with their little fingers that the shoemaker could not turn away his eyes in astonishment. They did not stop until all was done and stood finished on the table, and they ran quickly away.

Answer the following questions.

1. We know the shoemaker was very poor because he had _____ for one pair of shoes left.

2. Underline two expressions (four words each in the first paragraph) which mean the shoemaker was a good man.

3. Arrange the following sentences in the correct sequence:

   _____ The shoemaker was about to sit down to work.
   _____ The shoemaker examined the shoes closely.
   _____ The shoemaker was happy with the perfect finishing of the shoes.
   _____ The shoemaker said his prayers.

4. How do we know the shoes were really well made?

5. Which came first, the shoemaker's being 'honestly independent' or 'wealthy'?

6. Why did the shoemaker suggest to his wife that they should stay up in the night?

7. Where did the couple hide?

8. What did the two little men do?

9. The word _____ tells us that the little men came when it was all dark.

10. 'The shoemaker could not turn away his eyes in astonishment' means he

    a. was stunned
    b. was blinded
    c. became a statue

Read on:

Published in the *Grimm's Fairy Tales* (an 1812 anthology of German folklore), 'The Elves and the Shoemaker' tells of a poor shoemaker who goes off to bed, thinking of making one pair of leather shoes on waking up. The shoemaker and his wife are pleasantly surprised indeed when, in the morning, they see that the shoes are finished. They then decide to find out the mysterious source of the help they are getting.

The Slave and the Lion

Aesop

A slave ran away from his master, by whom he had been most cruelly treated and, in order to avoid capture, betook himself into the desert. As he wandered about in search of food and shelter, he came to a cave, which he entered and found to be unoccupied. Really, however, it was a lion's den, and almost immediately, to the horror of the wretched <u>fugitive</u>, the lion himself appeared.

The man gave himself up for lost, but, to his utter astonishment, the Lion, instead of springing upon him and devouring him, came and fawned upon him, at the same time whining and lifting up his paw. Observing it to be much swollen and inflamed, he examined it and found a large thorn embedded in the ball of the foot. He accordingly removed it and dressed the wound as well as he could, and in course of time it healed up completely. The Lion's gratitude was unbounded. He looked upon the man as his friend, and they shared the cave for some time together. A day came, however, when the slave began to long for the society of his fellow men, and he bade farewell to the lion and returned to the town.

Here he was presently recognised and carried off in chains to his former master, who resolved to make an example of him, and ordered that he should be thrown to the beasts at the next public spectacle in the theatre. On the fatal day, the beasts were loosed into the arena, and among the rest a lion of huge bulk and ferocious aspect, and then the wretched slave was cast in among them. What was the amazement of the spectators, when the lion after one glance bounded up to him and lay down at his feet with every expression of affected and delight! It was his old friend of the cave! The audience clamoured that the slave's life should be spared, and the governor of the town, marvelling at such gratitude and fidelity in a beast, decreed that both should receive their liberty.

Answer the following questions.

1. Why did the slave run away from his master?

2. Underline the phrase (three words in the first paragraph) which means 'looking for'.

3. The word 'unoccupied' tells us that

    a. there was no one else in the cave
    b. only animals lived in the cave
    c. the case was neat and clean

4. Connect the animals to their homes:

    a. lions   byre
    b. pigs   den
    c. cattle   burrow
    d. rabbits   sty

5. The fugitive as underlined in the first paragraph is referring to _____ _____.

6. What did the slave expect the lion to do?

7. What did the slave find in the paw of the lion?

8. What did the slave do to help the lion?

9. Underline the sentence in the second paragraph which shows the lion was very grateful.

10 The day when the slave would be thrown to the beast was described as 'a fatal' day because the slave was expected to _____ (one word).

11. The face of the lion was full of _____ and _____ when he saw the slave because

    a. it could play with him
    b. it was not hungry
    c. the man had saved him

12. In your own words, tell what happened to the slave and the lion at the end of the story.

Read on:

In this fable of Aesop, Androcles the slave befriends a lion by plucking a thorn out from its paw. The slave is later taken to the Colosseum to be thrown to a ferocious lion for the amusement of the emperor. The lion happens to recognise the man who has shown it kindness before and reciprocates with mercy and gratitude. Moved by the scene, the emperor sets Androcles and his new friend free together.

The Dog and the Cook

Aesop

A rich man once invited a number of his friends and acquaintances to a banquet. His dog thought it would be a good opportunity to invite another dog, a friend of his, so he went to him and said, 'My master is giving a feast: there'll be a fine spread, so come and dine with me tonight.'

The dog thus invited came, and when he saw the preparations being made in the kitchen, he said to himself, 'My word, I'm in luck: I'll take care to eat enough tonight to last me two or three days.' At the same time, he wagged his tail briskly, by way of showing his friend how delighted he was to have been asked. But just then the cook caught sight of him and, in his annoyance at seeing a strange dog in the kitchen, caught him up by the hind legs and threw him out of the window.

He had a nasty fall and limped away as quickly as he could, howling dismally. <u>Presently</u> some other dogs met him and said, 'Well, what sort of a dinner did you get?' to which he replied, 'I had a splendid time: the wine was so good, and I drank so much of it, that I really don't remember how I got out of the house!'

Be wary of favours bestowed at the expense of others.

Answer the following questions.

1. Whom was the rich man inviting to his banquet?

2. A banquet is

   a. a sports event
   b. a fun picnic
   c. a grand dinner

3. What was the relationship between the two dogs?

4. Underline the phrase (three words in the first paragraph) which means 'a lot of food will be served'.

5. 'My word' is an example of

   a. conjunction
   b. preposition
   c. interjection

6. How much did the dog that was invited plan to eat?

7. How did the dog that was invited show his pleasure?

8. How did the cook feel when he saw a strange dog in his kitchen? He felt _____.

9. What did the cook do to show his displeasure?

10. How do we know that the invited dog was badly hurt?

11. A synonym for 'presently' is

    a. at the same time
    b. soon
    c. nicely

12. Quote the line that states the moral of this fable.

Read on:

In the fable 'The Dog and the Cook', written by Aesop (620–546 BC), a dog is invited to share a sumptuous meal at a banquet held by the wealthy owner of his dog friend.

The visiting dog is eating to his heart's content when he is seen by the cook who, in fury and contempt, throws him out through the window. When asked by other dogs how dinner has been, he says, to save face, that he has eaten and drunk so much that he doesn't remember how he has gotten out of the house.

The Story of the Fisherman

Antoine Galland

Sire, there was once upon a time a fisherman so old and so poor that he could scarcely manage to support his wife and three children. He went every day to fish very early, and each day he made a rule not to throw his nets more than four times. He started out one morning by moonlight and came to the seashore. He undressed and threw his nets, and as he was drawing them towards the bank, he felt a great weight. He thought he had caught a large fish, and he felt very pleased. But a moment afterwards, seeing that instead of a fish he only had in his nets the carcase of an ass, he was much disappointed.

Vexed with having such a bad haul, when he had mended his nets, which the carcase of the ass had broken in several places, he threw them a second time. Drawing them in, he again felt a great weight, so he thought they were full of fish. But he only found a large basket full of rubbish. He was much annoyed.

'O Fortune,' he cried, 'do not trifle thus with me, a poor fisherman, who can hardly support his family!'

So saying, he threw away the rubbish, and after having washed his nets clean of the dirt, he threw them for the third time. But he only drew in stones, shells, and mud. He was almost in despair.

Then he threw his nets for the fourth time. When he thought he had a fish, he drew them in with a great deal of trouble. There was no fish, however, but he found a yellow pot, which by its weight seemed full of something, and he noticed that it was fastened and sealed with lead, with the impression of a seal. He was delighted. 'I will sell it to the founder,' he said. 'With the money I shall get for it I shall buy a measure of wheat.'

Answer the following questions.

1. The expression 'once upon a time' tells us the story happened _____ _____ _____ ago.

2. Underline the part of the sentence in the first paragraph that suggests the fisherman was very, very poor?

3. What was the rule of the fisherman when he went fishing?

4. When the fisherman felt a great weight for his first haul, he felt

   a. disappointed
   b. annoyed
   c. pleased

5. Match the correct synonyms:

   a. pleased   angry
   b. disappointed   delighted
   c. vexed   saddened
   d. annoyed   irritated

6. To whom was the fisherman talking when he said, 'Do not trifle thus with me.'

7. Underline the phrase (six words in the last paragraph) which means 'with a lot of effort'.

8. What did the fisherman do after throwing away the rubbish? Why did he do that?

9. What did the fisherman find in the fourth haul?

10. What was special with this last item the fisherman found?

11. What did the fisherman plan to do with the money he made?

12. Which of the four hauls would probably be the lightest?

   a. the first haul
   b. the second haul
   c. the third haul
   d. the fourth haul

Read on:

In 'Arabian Nights: The Story of the Fisherman', a poor fisherman who goes fishing every day catches in his net a yellow pot, which has trapped in it for centuries a genie larger in size than any giants that have existed. The encounter with the genie almost costs the fisherman his life if not for the trick he plays on the genie himself.

The Journal: Or Birthday Gifts

Eliza Fenwick

Only one of these children went to school, and that was the eldest boy.

Laurence Clayton. The others were instructed by a governess at home. Laurence was a fine boy, the hope and pride of his family. For nine birthdays he had received gifts from the hand of his father as the reward of his good conduct, and now his tenth birthday was approaching, and Mr Clayton had heard so pleasing an account of Laurence from his schoolmaster that he said, besides the present he meant to give him, he would on the birthday grant any favour Laurence should ask of him.

A week only was wanting to complete Laurence's tenth year. Company was invited, and the young folks were all thinking and talking of the expected pleasures of that day—all but Laurence, who became pensive and silent, shunned his brothers and sisters, and even the presence of his father, to shut himself up in his own room, but, as he replied, when asked about his health, that he was very well, it was supposed that he was busy at his studies, and they still prepared for the birthday.

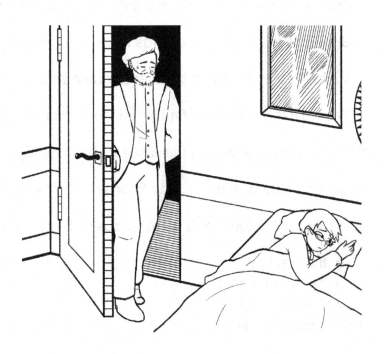

Answer the following questions.

1. How many children in the family went to school?

2. In modern days, when children are taught at home instead of going to school, it is called _____.

3. Underline the phrase (four words in the second paragraph) which suggests that the family had a lot of expectations of Laurence.

4. For what had Laurence received gifts from his father before his tenth birthday?

5. Was Mr Clayton happy with the schoolmaster's report on Laurence? How do we know?

6. It said in the passage that 'Company was invited'. It means

    a. relatives and friends were invited.
    b. Mr Clayton's colleagues were invited.
    c. teachers from school were invited.

7. Name two expected pleasures there would be at the birthday party.

8. Match the correct behaviour with the characters:

    a. Laurence   expecting fun
    b. the young folks   proud of his student
    c. Mr Clayton   ready to give two presents
    d. the schoolmaster   quiet and preoccupied

9. Where was Laurence found on his birthday? With whom was he supposed to be?

10. What was Laurence's excuse for being alone?

Read on:

'The Journal: Or Birthday Gifts' is one of the stories found in *The Bad Family and Other Stories* written by English writer Eliza Fenwick.

The story centres around the family of Mr Clayton, who always gives gifts to his children on their birthdays according to their overall performance at home and in school. When Lawrence, the eldest boy, turns ten, the birthday party is dampened by a series of incidents that have transpired that begs for a heartfelt confession and forgiveness.

The Story of Goldilocks and the Three Bears

Robert Southey

Once upon a time, there was a little girl named Goldilocks. She went for a walk in the forest. Pretty soon, she came upon a house. She knocked, and when no one answered, she walked right in.

At the table in the kitchen, there were three bowls of porridge. Goldilocks was hungry. She tasted the porridge from the first bowl.

'This porridge is too hot!' she exclaimed.

So she tasted the porridge from the second bowl.

'This porridge is too cold,' she said.

So she tasted the last bowl of porridge.

'Ahhh, this porridge is just right,' she said happily, and she ate it all up.

After she'd eaten the three bears' breakfasts, she decided she was feeling a little tired. So she walked into the living room where she saw three chairs. Goldilocks sat in the first chair to rest.

'This chair is too big!' she exclaimed.

So she sat in the second chair.

'This chair is too big, too!' she whined.

So she tried the last and smallest chair.

'Ahhh, this chair is just right,' she sighed. But just as she settled down into the chair to rest, it broke into pieces!

Goldilocks was very tired by this time. She went upstairs to the bedroom. She lay down in the first bed, but it was too hard. Then she lay in the second bed, but it was too soft. Then she lay down in the third bed, and it was just right. Goldilocks fell asleep.

As she was sleeping, the three bears came home.

'Someone's been eating my porridge,' growled Papa Bear.

Answer the following questions.

1. Which words tell us that the story happened a long time ago?

2. Underline the expression (two words in the first paragraph) which tells us that Goldilocks found the house unexpectedly.

3. How did Goldilocks find the first two bowls of porridge?

4. Did Goldilocks feel tired before or after eating the porridge?

5. Instead of using the verb 'said', the writer used verbs like _____, _____ and _____ to express the different emotions of the speaker.

6. Were the bedrooms on the ground floor? How do you know?

7. What was common among the porridge, the chair and the bed as far as Goldilocks was concerned?

8. Fill in the blanks with the correct tenses based on the verb 'lay' as used in the story.

   a. When I feel tired, I'd like to _____ down.
   b. She has _____ in bed for a while, hasn't she?

9. Give two homonyms for the word 'too'.

10. How do we know Papa Bear was angry?

11. Arrange the following sentences in the correct sequence:

   _____ Goldilocks tried out the chairs.
   _____ Goldilocks felt tired and needed to rest.
   _____ Goldilocks went for a walk in the forest.
   _____ Goldilocks tried out the porridge.

Read on:

Authored by Robert Southey and published in 1837, the original story of 'Goldilocks and the Three Bears' tells of an old woman who comes upon a house in the forest while the owners, three bears, were out and about. The old woman enters the house and messes with their bowls of porridge, chairs and beds. Upon being discovered by the bears, she runs out and is never seen again.

In 1849, twelve years after Southey's story was published, Joseph Cundell, another writer, changed the old woman to a little girl in his version of the story.

Buster Bear Goes Fishing

Thornton W. Burgess

<u>Buster Bear</u> yawned as he lay on his comfortable bed of leaves and watched the first early morning sunbeams creeping through the Green Forest to chase out the Black Shadows. Once more he yawned, and slowly got to his feet and shook himself. Then he walked over to a big pine tree, stood up on his hind legs, reached as high up on the trunk of the tree as he could and scratched the bark with his great claws. After that, he yawned until it seemed as if his jaws would crack and then sat down to think what he wanted for breakfast.

While he sat there, trying to make up his mind what would taste best, he was listening to the sounds that told of the waking of all the little people who live in the Green Forest. He heard <u>Sammy Jay</u> way off in the distance screaming, 'Thief! Thief!' and grinned. *I wonder,* thought Buster, *if someone has stolen Sammy's breakfast, or if he has stolen the breakfast of someone else. Probably he is the thief himself.*

He heard <u>Chatterer the Red Squirrel</u> scolding as fast as he could make his tongue go and working himself into a terrible rage. *Must be that Chatterer got out of bed the wrong way this morning,* thought he.

He heard <u>Blacky the Crow</u> cawing at the top of his lungs, and he knew by sounds that Blacky was getting into mischief of some kind. He heard the sweet voices of happy little singers, and they were good to hear. But most of all, he listened to a merry, low, silvery laugh that never stopped but went on and on until he just felt as if he must laugh too. It was the voice of the <u>Laughing Brook</u>. And as Buster listened, it suddenly came to him just what he wanted for breakfast.

'I'm going fishing,' said he in his deep grumbly-rumbly voice to no one in particular. 'Yes, Sit, I'm going fishing. I want some fat trout for my breakfast.'

He shuffled along over to the Laughing Brook and straight to a little pool of which he knew, and as he drew near he took the greatest care not to make the teeniest, weeniest bit of noise. Now it just happened that early as he was, someone was before Buster Bear.

Answer the following questions.

1. The bed of Buster Bear was soft/hard as it was made of grass/leaves.

2. Why did Buster Bear reach high up on the big pine tree?

3. Buster Bear yawned _____ times before he sat down. He was probably still feeling _____.

4. Did Buster Bear know immediately what he would like for breakfast? Explain.

5. Matching:

   a. Sammy Jay   was getting into troublemaking.
   b. Chatterer the Red Squirrel   made a happy, low laugh.
   c. Blacky the Crow   cried, 'Thief! Thief!'.
   d. Laughing Brook   decided to go fishing.
   e. Buster Bear   started getting angry.

6. Buster believed that the one who cried, 'Thief! Thief!' was _____ _____ himself.

7. Underline the expression (seven words between paragraphs 2 and 4) which means 'would be in a bad mood the whole day'.

8. When a person shouts at the top of his lungs, he shouts

   a. very angrily
   b. very loudly
   c. very clearly

9. What did Buster Bear finally decide to have for breakfast?

10. True or False:

   a. Buster Bear walked to the Laughing Brook in brisk steps. _____
   b. Buster Bear tried not to make any noise. _____
   c. Buster Bear was not the first one to arrive at the brook. _____

Read on:

In Thornton W. Burgess's 'Buster Bear Goes Fishing', published in 1920, the reader finds Buster Bear awake in the Green Forest, contemplating about breakfast as he is hungry. He hears the sounds made by different animals, his coinhabitants among bushes and trees, as well as the singing of the birds. Suddenly what comes to Buster Bear's mind is having some fish, some fat trout to be exact, for his fish bowl.

What Is Pink?

Christina Rossetti

What is pink? A rose is pink

By the fountains' brink

What is red? A poppy's red

In its barley bed.

What is blue? The sky is blue

Where the clouds float through.

What is white? A swan is white

Sailing in the light.

What is yellow? Pears are yellow,

Rich and ripe and mellow.

What is green? The grass is green,

With small flowers between.

What is violet? Clouds are violet

In the summer twilight.

What is orange? Why, an orange,

Just an orange!

Answer the following questions.

1. The poet who wrote 'What Is Pink' is _____ _____.

2. How many stanzas are there in this poem?

3. Give two examples of rhymes used in this poem.

4. True or False:

    a. A rose is found growing on the side of the mountain. _____
    b. The sky where the clouds float through is blue. _____

5. Use four adjectives to describe the pear.

6. How many questions are asked? Are these questions all answered?

7. Which is the funniest line in this poem? Why do you think so?

8. Give another title for this poem.

Read on:

Christina Rossetti's poem 'What Is Pink?' is a simple poem that describes various colours and their associations with nature. Only orange stands out in the sense that only its basic quality is portrayed.

All in all, Rossetti is encouraging us readers to dwell deeper into what we see around us positively and discern how they are connected though being different, separate entities.

The Little Mermaid Story

Hans Christian Andersen

Far out in the sea where the water was very deep, the Sea King ruled the undersea world.

In the deepest spot of the sea was his castle. The walls were made of blue coral. On the roof were shells that opened and closed when the water passed by. And that was where the Sea King lived with his mother and four daughters, each one born a year apart.

The youngest of the four princesses was the Little Mermaid. She spent much of her time swimming to ships that had fallen to the bottom of the sea. The ships held treasures from the world above. She would fill her arms and set up her collection here and there. All the while we would sing. As she did, fish circled around to hear her, for the Little Mermaid's voice was the most beautiful one under the sea.

The girls knew that when they turned fifteen, they could swim up to the surface for the first time. It would be a long time that the Little Mermaid had to wait, as she was the youngest! So she made her grandmother tell her all about life up on land: tales about ships and towns, and every bit of stories about humans that <u>she</u> knew.

Soon the eldest sister turned fifteen. She was the first to be allowed to rise up to the surface. When she came back, she had many wonders to tell her sisters about! She told about resting on soft white sand. High above was a deep blue sky with puffy white clouds. Later the sun set, she said, and the whole sky turned gold and red. She had watched the birds fly high above her, dipping and making turns in the red-and-gold sky.

Answer the following questions.

1. According to the story, _____ _____ _____ ruled the undersea world.

2. What two things was the Sea King's castle made of?

3. True or False:

   a. Besides the Sea King himself, all the other members in the family were females. ____
   b. All the girls in the family were of the same age. ____

4. Why was the Little Mermaid interested in visiting the ships that had fallen to the bottom of the sea?

5. Why would the Little Mermaid attract other fish while she was singing?

6. Could the mermaids swim up to the surface when they were ten years old? Why or why not?

7. Among the four mermaids, why would the Little Mermaid have to wait the longest time before she could swim to the surface of the sea?

8. Who is 'she' in the last line of the fourth paragraph referring to?

9. Underline the part of the sentence which tells us that the eldest mermaid had a lot of stories to tell when she returned from the surface of the sea.

10. What didn't the eldest sister see?

   a. soft white sand
   b. the deep blue sky
   c. birds singing
   d. the gold-and-red sky

Read on:

Written by Hans Christian Andersen and published in 1845, *The Little Mermaid* is a tragic story of Danish origin but blessed with a happy ending. It follows the adventurous journey of a young mermaid who is willing to give up her life in the sea in exchange for a human soul. The themes of this story include selflessness, freedom and immortality.

The Poor Sick Mother

Sophie Ségur

Henry walked a long, long time, but he walked in vain, for he saw that he was no farther from the foot of the mountain and no nearer to the summit than he had been when he crossed the river. Any other child would have retraced his steps, but the brave little Henry would not allow himself to be discouraged. Notwithstanding his extreme fatigue, he walked on twenty-one days without seeming to make any advance. At the end of this time, he was no more discouraged than at the close of the first day.

'If I am obliged to walk a hundred years,' he said aloud, 'I will go on till I reach the summit.'

'You have then a great desire to arrive there, little boy?' said an old man, looking at him maliciously and standing just in his path. 'What are you seeking at the top of this mountain?'

'The plant of life, my good sir, to save the life of my dear mother who is about to die.'

The little old man shook his head, rested his little pointed chin on the top of his gold-headed cane and after having a long time regarded Henry, he said:

'Your sweet and fresh face pleases me, my boy. I am one of the genii of this mountain. I will allow you to advance on condition that you will gather all my wheat, that you will beat it out, make it turn into flour and then into bread. When you have gathered, beaten, ground and cooked it, then call me. You will find all the necessary implements in the ditch near you. The fields of wheat are before you and cover the mountain.'

The old man disappeared, and Henry gazed in terror at the immense fields of wheat which were spread out before him. But he soon mastered this feeling of discouragement—took off his vest, scribed a scythe and commenced cutting the wheat diligently. This occupied him a hundred and ninety-five days and nights.

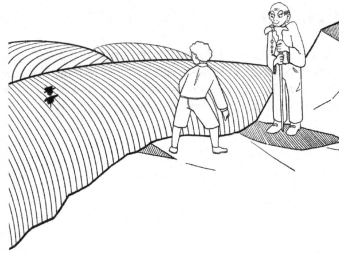

Answer the following questions.

1. Henry had walked from _____ _____ of the mountain and was trying to reach the _____.

2. Underline the phrase (two words in the first paragraph) which means 'without success'.

3. How was Henry different from the other children?

4. Henry said even if he had to walk a hundred years, he would go on till he reached the summit. This tells us that Henry

  a. would never get tired
  b. would not give up easily
  c. would continue to walk after reaching the summit

5. Where did Henry meet the old man? What word makes you immediately think he was not a good old man?

6. What was Henry's reason for wanting to reach the summit?

7. What was the old man holding in his hand?

8. What were Henry's tasks in order to advance?

9. What struck Henry that what the old man asked for was a daunting task?

10. Is this story fiction or nonfiction?

Read on:

'The Poor Sick Mother', one of the stories found in *Good Little Henry—The Harvest,* was written by Comtesse de Segur and published in 1920 in *Old French Fairy Tales.* In the story, a little boy, Henry, who loves his sick and dying mother dearly, is ready to go and seek the plant of life to restore his mother to health. The danger Henry has to face and the daunting tasks he has to accomplish put, without doubt, the little boy's willpower and filial love for his mother to the ultimate test.

Hansel and Gretel

The Brothers Grimm

The moon shone brightly, and the white pebbles which lay in front of the house glittered like real silver pennies. Hansel stooped and studded the little pocket of his coat with as many as he could get in. Then he went back and said to Gretel, 'Be comforted, dear little sister, and sleep in peace, God will not forsake us,' and he lay down again in his bed.

When day dawned, but before the sun had risen, the woman came and awoke the two children, saying, 'Get up, you sluggards. We are going into the forest to fetch wood.' She gave each a little piece of bread and said, 'There is something for your dinner, but do not eat it up before then, for you will get nothing else.'

Gretel put the bread under her apron, as Handsel had the pebbles in his pocket. Then they all set out together on the way to the forest.

When they had walked a short time, Hansel stood still and peeped back at the house, and did so again and again. His father said, 'Hansel, what are you looking at there and staying behind for? Pay attention, and do not forget how to use your legs.'

'Ah, Father,' said Hansel, 'I am looking at my little white cat, which is sitting up on the roof, and wants to say goodbye to me.'

The wife said, 'Fool, that is not your little cat, that is the morning sun which is shining on the chimneys.'

Hansel, however, had not been looking back at the cat, but had been constantly throwing one of the white pebble stones out of his pocket on the road.

When they had reached the middle of the forest, the father said, 'Now, children, pile up some wood, and I will light a fire that you may not be cold.'

Answer the following questions.

1. Why were the white pebbles in front of the house glittering?

2. What were they glittering like?

3. What was the relationship between Hansel and Gretel?

4. How do we know the story is set very early in the morning?

5. The word 'sluggards' means

    a. little insects
    b. lazy people
    c. smart children

6. How many pieces of bread did the two children get all together?

7. Did Hansel turn around to look at the house just once or many times? How do you know?

8. Do you think Hansel's mother loved him a lot? How do you know?

9. The little cat was actually the _____ _____.

10. What was Hansel actually doing when he kept looking back?

11. True or False:

    a. Gretel put bread in her apron. _____
    b. Gretel put bread in her pocket. _____
    c. Hansel put pebbles in his pocket. _____
    d. Hansel put pebbles in his jacket. _____

Read on:

In 'Hansel and Gretel', one of the famous stories published by German Brothers Grimm in 1812, a brother and sister are abandoned by their parents in the forest. They are then lured by a wicked witch to her house made of gingerbread, cake and candy. In the end, the two little protagonists manage to escape with the witch's treasure.

The Velveteen Rabbit

Margery Williams Bianco

This began another happy time for Velveteen Rabbit. Each night the Boy would hold Velveteen Rabbit close in his arms. In the morning, the Boy would show Velveteen Rabbit how to make rabbit holes under the sheets. If the Boy went outside to a picnic, or to the park, Velveteen Rabbit would come with him too.

After a while, with the hugging and holding, much of Velveteen Rabbit's fur got matted down. Its pink nose grew less pink with all the Boy's kisses. But Velveteen Rabbit did not care. It was happy.

One day the Boy became sick. His forehead got very hot. The doctor came and went. Nana walked back and forth in fear. Day after day, the Boy stayed in bed. There was nothing for Velveteen Rabbit to do but to stay in bed, too, day after day.

Then at last, the Boy got better. Such joy in the house! The doctor said the Boy must go to the shore. *How wonderful!* thought Velveteen Rabbit. Many times the Boy had talked happily about the shore and told of its white sands and big blue ocean.

'What about his old bunny?' Nana asked the doctor.

'That old thing?' said the doctor. 'It's full of scarlet fever germs. Burn it at once! Get him a new bunny.'

So Velveteen Rabbit was thrown into a sack along with the Boy's bedsheets and old clothes and a lot of junk. The sack was carried to the backyard. The gardener was told to burn the whole thing.

Answer the following questions.

1. In the first line, which word tells us that Velveteen Rabbit has had a happy time before?

2. What would the Boy show Velveteen Rabbit in the morning?

3. What was the reason Velveteen Rabbit's fur was matted down?

4. Why didn't Velveteen Rabbit care that his nose was growing less pink?

5. How do we know the Boy had a fever?

6. Which phrase tells us that the Boy was sick for a while?

7. What did Velveteen Rabbit do when the Boy was sick?

8. Where did the doctor suggest the Boy should go?

9. Did the Boy get a new bunny? Yes/No/The answer is not there

10. Why did the doctor want to get rid of Velveteen Rabbit?

11. Arrange the following sentences in the correct sequence:

_____ Velveteen Rabbit's fur got worn out.
_____ Velveteen Rabbit was thrown into a sack.
_____ The Boy became sick.
_____ The Boy spent a lot of time with Velveteen Rabbit.

Read on:

In the British children's book *The Velveteen Rabbit*, written by Margery Williams and illustrated by William Nicholson, a little boy truly grows to love a stuffed rabbit, which he received as a Christmas present.

Being abandoned with other toys after the boy gets very sick, the rabbit desires to become real. With the help of the nursery magic fairy, it is taken to the forest, where it changes into a real rabbit and returns to visit its former owner the following spring.

Cinderella

Charles Perrault

'Wait!' called the Prince. He picked up her glass slipper and rushed out the door. He looked around but could not see her blue dress anywhere. 'This is all I have left from her,' he said, looking down at the glass slipper. He saw that it was made in a special way, to fit a foot like none other. 'Somewhere there is the other glass slipper,' he said. 'And when I find it, I will find her, too. Then I will ask her to be my bride!'

From hut to hut, from house to house, went the Prince. One young woman after another tried to fit her foot inside the glass slipper. But none could fit. And so the Prince soon <u>moved on</u>.

At last the Prince came to Cinderella's house.

'He is coming!' called one stepsister as she looked out the window.

'At the door!' screamed the other stepsister.

'Quick!' yelled the stepmother. 'Get ready! One of you must be the one to fit your foot in that slipper. No matter what!'

The Prince knocked. The stepmother flew open the door. 'Come in!' she said. 'I have two lovely daughters for you to see.'

The first stepsister tried to place her foot in the glass slipper. She tried hard, but it just would not fit. Then the second stepsister tried to fit her foot inside. She tried and tried with all her might too. But no dice.

'Are there no other young women in the house?' said the Prince.

'None,' said the stepmother.

'Then I must go,' said the Prince.

'Maybe there is one more,' said Cinderella, stepping into the room.

'I thought <u>you</u> said there were no other young women here,' said the Prince.

'None who matter!' said the stepmother in a hiss.

'Come here,' said the Prince.

Answer the following questions.

1. If the Prince could see the blue dress, it means he could see _____.

2. What was so special about the slipper?

    (a) _____

    (b) _____

3. What did the Prince want to do when he found the owner of the glass slipper?

4. Underline two phrases (eight words in paragraphs 1 to 2) which tell us that the Prince looked for the owner of the glass slipper thoroughly.

5. 'Moved on' means

    a. continued his search
    b. went back to the palace
    c. walked slowly

6. Who was the first one to see the Prince coming?

7. Give two words used in the passage in place of 'said loudly'.

8. Which sentence (three words) tells us that the stepmother was determined to get one of her daughters to fit the slipper?

9. The pronoun 'you' in the fourth last line is referring to _____ _____.

10. How do you think the story will end?

Read on:

First recorded as an old tale originating from Egypt, 'Cinderella' was first recorded by a Greek geographer in the first century B.C.

In this well-known fairy tale, also known as 'The Little Glass Slipper', a simple and kind maiden suffers great unjust treatment imposed by her stepmother and two stepsisters. The appearance of her fairy godmother enables Cinderella to be freed of her contemptible stepfamily and, with the help of a glass slipper, have her dreams of marrying the prince come true.

Beauty and the Beast

Gabrielle-Suzanne de Villeneuve

Once upon a time, there was a very rich man who lived with his three daughters. The two elder daughters laughed at anyone who did not dress as well as they did. If they were not going to a ball, they were shopping for as many fine dresses and hats as they could carry home.

The youngest daughter, Beauty, liked to read most of all. 'No one will want you!' her two elder sisters said, and they laughed. 'Look at your hair—you look like a servant girl!' Beauty did not know why they talked to her in a mean way. But she said nothing.

One day, the father got some very bad news. He had spent all of his money on a ship that he had sent out to sea for trade. Now he learned that the ship was gone. Everything on it was lost! All at once, the rich father became as poor as poor could be.

The family could no longer stay in their big house. The house, its fine tables and chairs, and all of their fine things had to be sold.

All the father had left was a little hut deep in the woods, so that was where he and his three daughters had to move. Living in the hut in the woods was hard work. Each day a fire had to be started, meals cooked, the place cleaned up, the garden tended and things fixed when they broke. Now that the family was poor, you might think the two elder sisters would help out with the chores. <u>Think again.</u>

'She looks like such a mess,' they said, turning up their noses at Beauty. 'She might as well serve us.' And so Beauty did all the hard work.

And then—good news!—the father's ship came to shore!

'Daughters,' said the happy father, 'I am going to town. Tell me what fine gift I can bring back for you.'

'Bring me the finest dress from the finest shop,' said the eldest sister.

'I want one just like it,' said the middle sister.

'And you, Beauty?' said he.

'All I want, Father,' said she, 'is a single rose.'

Answer the following questions.

1. What behaviour tells us that the elder two sisters were vain?

2. Did Beauty understand her sisters? How do you know?

3. The adjective to describe the elder two daughters:

    a. snobbish
    b. curious
    c. patient
    d. passionate

4. What was the bad news that the father received one day?

5. Find a simile in the third paragraph of this story.

6. What happened to the furniture and all the fine things in the house?

7. Which sentence tells us that it wasn't easy living in the hut in the woods?

8. 'Think again'. What does this short sentence imply?

9. What was the good news that came one day?

10. What did the father promise the girls before he left for town?

11. What did Beauty want for a gift? What adjective that can be used to describe Beauty is:

    a. vain
    b. dull
    c. modest

Read on:

Written by Gabrielle-Suzanne Barbot de Villeneuve and published in 1740, 'Beauty and the Beast' is a traditional fairy tale about a handsome prince cursed by an enchantress to live alone as a monstrous beast. He can only undo the curse and regain his looks and humanity by winning the true love of a maiden.

The story begins with the introduction of a family with a father and three daughters, of whom the youngest, called Beauty, already exhibits the character of a gentle, humble soul.

My Father's Dragon

My Father Meets the Cat
Ruth Stiles Gannett

One cold rainy day when my father was a little boy, he met an old alley cat on his street. The cat was very drippy and uncomfortable, so my father said, 'Wouldn't you like to come home with me?

This surprised the cat—she had never before met anyone who cared about old alley cats—but she said, 'I'd be very much obliged if I could sit by a warm furnace, and perhaps have a saucer of milk.'

'We have a very nice furnace to sit by,' said my father, 'and I'm sure my mother has an extra saucer of milk.'

My father and the cat became good friends, but my father's mother was very upset about the cat. She hated cats, particularly ugly, old alley cats. 'Elmer Elevator,' she said to my father, 'if you think I'm going to give that cat a saucer of milk, you're very wrong. Once you start feeding stray alley cats, you might as well expect to feed every stray in town, and I am *not* going to do it!'

This made my father very sad, and he apologised to the cat because his mother had been so rude. He told the cat to stay anyway and that somehow he would bring her a saucer of milk each day. My father fed the cat for three weeks, but one day his mother found the cat's saucer in the cellar, and she was extremely angry. She whipped my father and threw the cat out of the door, but later on my father sneaked out and found the cat. Together they went for a walk in the park and tried to think of nice things to talk about. My father said, 'When I grow up I'm going to have an airplane. Wouldn't it be wonderful to fly just anywhere you might think of!'

'Would you like to fly very, very much?' asked the cat.

'I certainly would. I'd do anything if I could fly.'

Answer the following questions.

1. What was the weather like the day the writer's father met the alley cat?

2. Does an alley cat have a home to go back to?

3. What surprised the cat?

4. Match the words with their meaning:

    a. drippy   grateful
    b. obliged   especially
    c. apologised   said sorry
    d. particularly   weak
    e. extremely   very

5. What did the cat want to do in the writer's father's house?

6. Which three words tell us that the writer's grandmother did not like cats at all?

7. Why didn't the writer's grandmother want to feed stray cats?

8. Why did the writer's father apologise to the cat?

9. What was the writer's grandmother's reaction upon finding the cat's saucer in the cellar?

10. What did the writer's father want to own one day?

11. What part of the story could be real? What part of the story could not be real?

Read on:

Authored by Ruth Stiles Gannett and published in 1948, *My Father's Dragon* is the first book of a trilogy which follows the adventures of Elmer Elevator, who runs away from home to rescue a chained-up baby dragon on Wild Island. The themes of bravery and friendship are warmed by elements of fun and humour throughout the story. It is a book with beautiful illustrations by Ruth Chrisman Gannett, the aunt of the writer.

Answers

Note to teachers

1. Some of the questions require students to re-examine the text for answers.
2. Some of the questions require students to think to arrive at an answer.
3. Other questions require common sense and some background knowledge. Answers to these questions are often open-ended (shown as 'multiple answers allowed').

Ali Baba and the Forty Thieves

1. brothers; Persia
2. a. wealthy
3. No—but the wife of Ali Baba was as poor as himself.
4. a woodcutter
5. approaching
6. many bags of solid coins
7. to load them with more treasures
8. Yes—he found more treasures than he expected
9. d. greed
10. the sound of horses' feet

Belling the Cat

1. 'Long ago'
2. the Cat
3. 'Some said this and some said that.'
4. He made a proposal.
5. 'sly' and 'treacherous'
6. signal; approach; escape
7. a small bell and a ribbon
8. 'with general applause'
9. no one
10. 3 1 4 2
11. fable

Twinkle, Twinkle, Little Star

1. b. a child
2. a diamond
3. blazing
4. the sun
5. he could see where to go
6. 'How could he see where to go,
    If you did not twinkle so?'

7. c. It comes out in the daytime to twinkle.
8. No—'Though I know not what you are.'
9. 3 1 4 2

The Frog Prince

1. bonnet; clogs
2. a. a rose
3. 'her favourite plaything'
4. No—only gold in colour
5. It fell down into the spring.
6. No—it was too deep
7. c. the golden ball
8. 'bitterly'
9. a. True
   b. False
10. She thought the frog could never get out of the spring to visit her.

Winnie the Pooh

1. a. very unhappy
2. No
3. on the other side of the river
4. c. 'Happy birthday'
5. excited
6. a little present
7. a snuffling sound
8. a Useful Pot; for putting things in
9. Yes—he became quite excited
10. balloons are much too big to go into Pots

The Elves and the Shoemaker

1. leather
2. 'commended himself to God' and 'had a good conscience'
3. 2 3 4 1
4. There was not one bad stitch.
5. 'honestly independent'
6. he wanted to see who it was that lent them the helping hand
7. in a corner of the room behind some clothes which were hanging up there
8. They stitched, sewed and hammered.
9. midnight
10. a. was stunned

The Slave and the Lion

1. he had been most cruelly treated
2. 'in search of'
3. a. there was no one else in the cave
4. a. lions → den

    b. pigs → sty

    c. cattle → byre

    d. rabbits → burrow
5. the slave
6. to spring upon him
7. a large thorn
8. removed the large thorn and dressed the wound as well as he could
9. 'The Lion's gratitude was unbounded.'
10. die
11. affection; delight

    c. the man had saved him
12. both slave and lion were free

The Dog and the Cook

1. friends and acquaintances
2. c. a grand dinner
3. friends
4. a fine spread
5. c. interjection
6. enough to last him two to three days
7. He wagged his tail briskly.
8. annoyed
9. He caught the strange dog by his hind legs and threw him out of the window.
10. He limped away.
11. b. soon
12. 'Be wary of favours bestowed at the expense of others.'

The Story of the Fisherman

1. a long time
2. 'he could scarcely manage to support his wife and their children'
3. not to throw his nets more than four times a day
4. c. pleased
5. a. pleased → delighted

    b. disappointed → saddened

    c. vexed → angry

    d. annoyed → irritated

6. to 'Fortune'
7. 'with a great deal of trouble'
8. washed his nets clean of the dirt; it's not nice to fish with a dirty net
9. a yellow pot
10. It was fastened and sealed with lead, with the impression of a seal.
11. to buy a measure of wheat
12. d. the fourth haul

The Journal: Or Birthday Gifts

1. one
2. homeschooling/home education
3. the hope and pride
4. his good conduct
5. Yes—besides the present he meant to give Laurence, Mr. Clayton would on his birthday grant any favour Laurence should ask of him
6. a. relatives and friends were invited.
7. playing games/eating snacks/eating birthday cake/getting party gifts (multiple answers accepted)
8. a. Laurence → quiet and preoccupied
   b. the young folks → expecting fun
   c. Mr Clayton → ready to give two presents
   d. the schoolmaster → proud of his student
9. in his own room; his brothers, sisters and father
10. He claimed he was busy with his studies.

The Story of Goldilocks and the Three Bears

1. 'Once upon a time'
2. 'came upon'
3. The first bowl of porridge was too hot and the second bowl, too cold.
4. after eating the porridge
5. exclaimed; whined; sighed
6. No—she went upstairs
7. The first and second ones were not good enough. The last ones were what Goldilocks picked.
8. a. lie
   b. lain
9. to; two
10. He growled.
11. 3 4 1 2

Buster Bear Goes Fishing

1. soft; leaves

2. he wanted to scratch the bark with his great paws
3. three; tired / sleepy
4. No—he was trying to make up his mind what would taste best
5. a. Sammy Jay → cried, 'Thief! Thief!'
   b. Chatterer the Red Squirrel → started getting angry.
   c. Blacky the Crow → was getting into troublemaking.
   d. Laughing Brook → made a happy, low laugh.
   e. Buster Bear → decided to go fishing.
6. the thief
7. 'got out of bed the wrong way'
8. b. very loudly
9. some fat trout
10. a. False
    b. True
    c. True

What Is Pink?

1. Christina Rossetti
2. one
3. pink; brink / red; bed / blue; through / white; light / yellow; mellow / green; between / violet; twilight (any two examples)
4. a. False
   b. True
5. yellow; rich; ripe; mellow
6. eight; yes
7. 'What is orange? Why an orange, Just an orange!'
   all the other colours describe something else, but the colour orange describes the fruit itself
8. Colours (multiple answers accepted)

The Little Mermaid Story

1. the Sea King
2. blue coral and shells
3. a. True
   b. False
4. the ships held treasures from the world above
5. her voice was the most beautiful one under the sea
6. No—they had to be fifteen
7. she was the youngest
8. Little Mermaid's grandmother
9. 'she had many wonders to tell her sisters about'
10. c. birds singing

The Poor Sick Mother

1. the foot; summit
2. 'in vain'
3. Any other child would have retraced his steps, but Henry would not allow himself to be discouraged.
4. b. would not give up easily
5. in his path on his walk to the summit; maliciously
6. to seek the plant of life to save the life of his dear mother who was about to die
7. a gold-headed cane
8. to gather all the old man's wheat, beat it out, make it into flour and make the flour into bread
9. the sight of the immense fields of wheat
10. fiction

Hansel and Gretel

1. the moon shone brightly
2. real silver pennies
3. brother and sister / siblings
4. the day dawned
5. b. lazy people
6. two pieces
7. many times—'he did so again and again'
8. No—she gave them each only a piece of bread / she called them sluggards and Hansel, a fool
9. morning sun
10. He had been constantly throwing one of the white pebble stones out of his pocket on the road.
11. a. True
    b. False
    c. True
    d. True (the pocket was in his jacket)

The Velveteen Rabbit

1. 'another'
2. how to make rabbit holes under the sheets
3. the hugging and holding
4. it was happy
5. His head got very hot.
6. 'Day after day'
7. It stayed in bed too.
8. the shore

9. The answer is not there
10. it was full of scarlet fever germs
11. 2 4 3 1

Cinderella

1. Cinderella
2. a. it was made of glass
   b. it would fit only one person
3. He wanted her to be his bride. / He wanted to marry her.
4. 'From hut to hut, from house to house'
5. a. continued his search
6. one of the stepsisters
7. 'screamed' and 'yelled'
8. 'No matter what!'
9. the stepmother
10. The Prince will marry Cinderella. / It will end happily.

Beauty and the Beast

1. If they were not going to a ball, they were shopping for as many fine dresses and hats as they could carry home.
2. No—Beauty did not know why they talked to her in a mean way
3. a. snobbish
4. The ship which he had spent all his money on was gone, and everything on it was lost.
5. 'as poor as poor could be'
6. They had to be sold.
7. 'Living in the hut in the woods was hard work.'
8. we readers are wrong—the two sisters would not help out
9. The father's ship came to shore.
10. a fine gift
11. a single rose; c. modest

My Father's Dragon

1. cold and rainy
2. No—sleeps in the street
3. that the writer invited her to go home with him
4. a. drippy → weak
   b. obliged → grateful
   c. apologised → said sorry
   d. particularly → especially
   e. extremely → very
5. to sit by a warm furnace and have a saucer of milk
6. 'She hated cats.'

7. she didn't want to feed every stray (cat) in town
8. his mother had been so rude
9. She was extremely angry.
10. an airplane
11. Real - feeding cats
    Not real - the cat talking
    (multiple answers accepted)

Printed in the United States
by Baker & Taylor Publisher Services